35
THOM

Second baseman Eddie Collins

Outfielder Andrew Benintendi

THE STORY OF THE

CHICAGO WHITE SOX

JOE TISCHLER

CREATIVE SPORTS

Pitcher Lucas Giolito

CREATIVE EDUCATION / CREATIVE PAPERBACKS

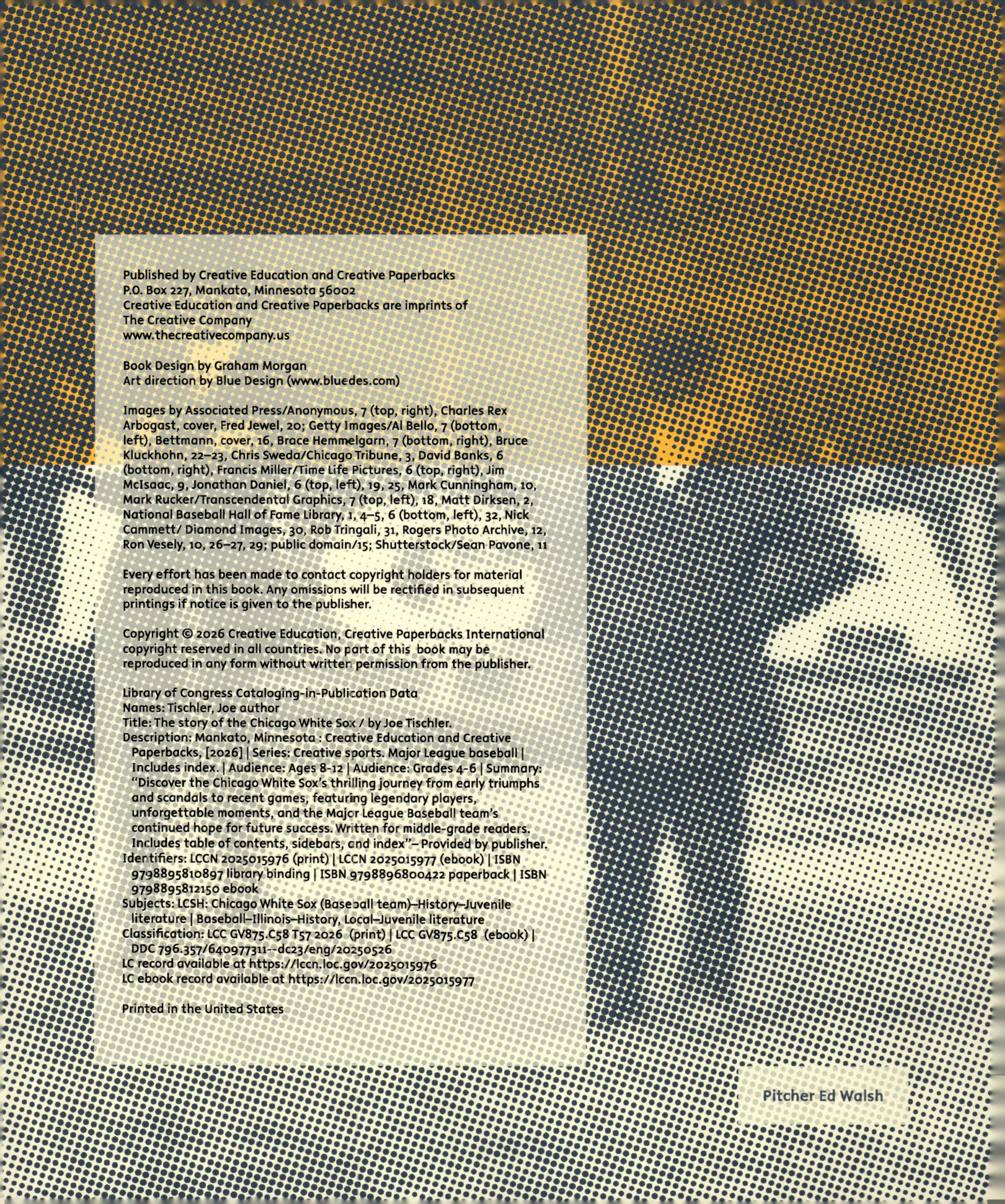

Published by Creative Education and Creative Paperbacks
P.O. Box 227, Mankato, Minnesota 56002
Creative Education and Creative Paperbacks are imprints of
The Creative Company
www.thecreativecompany.us

Book Design by Graham Morgan
Art direction by Blue Design (www.bluedes.com)

Images by Associated Press/Anonymous, 7 (top, right), Charles Rex Arbogast, cover, Fred Jewel, 20; Getty Images/Al Bello, 7 (bottom, left), Bettmann, cover, 16, Brace Hemmelgarn, 7 (bottom, right), Bruce Kluckhohn, 22–23, Chris Sweda/Chicago Tribune, 3, David Banks, 6 (bottom, right), Francis Miller/Time Life Pictures, 6 (top, right), Jim McIsaac, 9, Jonathan Daniel, 6 (top, left), 19, 25, Mark Cunningham, 10, Mark Rucker/Transcendental Graphics, 7 (top, left), 18, Matt Dirksen, 2, National Baseball Hall of Fame Library, 1, 4–5, 6 (bottom, left), 32, Nick Cammett/ Diamond Images, 30, Rob Tringali, 31, Rogers Photo Archive, 12, Ron Vesely, 10, 26–27, 29; public domain/15; Shutterstock/Sean Pavone, 11

Library of Congress Cataloging-in-Publication Data
Names: Tischler, Joe author
Title: The story of the Chicago White Sox / by Joe Tischler.
Description: Mankato, Minnesota : Creative Education and Creative Paperbacks, [2026] | Series: Creative sports. Major League baseball | Includes index. | Audience: Ages 8-12 | Audience: Grades 4-6 | Summary: "Discover the Chicago White Sox's thrilling journey from early triumphs and scandals to recent games, featuring legendary players, unforgettable moments, and the Major League Baseball team's continued hope for future success. Written for middle-grade readers. Includes table of contents, sidebars, and index"– Provided by publisher.
Identifiers: LCCN 2025015976 (print) | LCCN 2025015977 (ebook) | ISBN 9798895810897 library binding | ISBN 9798896800422 paperback | ISBN 9798895812150 ebook
Subjects: LCSH: Chicago White Sox (Baseball team)–History–Juvenile literature | Baseball–Illinois–History, Local–Juvenile literature
Classification: LCC GV875.C58 T57 2026 (print) | LCC GV875.C58 (ebook) | DDC 796.357/640977311--dc23/eng/20250526
LC record available at https://lccn.loc.gov/2025015976
LC ebook record available at https://lccn.loc.gov/2025015977

Printed in the United States

Pitcher Ed Walsh

CONTENTS

EXTRA INNINGS

RECORD PERFECTION

Chicago White Sox starting pitcher Mark Buehrle was no stranger to throwing no-hitters. In an April 2007 game against the Texas Rangers, the left-hander threw his first career no-hitter in a 6–0 White Sox win. He was very close to throwing a perfect game. That is where a pitcher does not allow a single opposing batter to reach base in a nine-inning game. The only base runner he allowed was on a walk to Sammy Sosa in the fifth inning. Buehrle proceeded to quickly pick him off first base.

Buehrle was having a good year with the White Sox in 2009. He improved his record to 10–3 after a win over the Baltimore Orioles on July 18. Buehrle threw seven and one-third innings, allowing just one run on eight hits. He retired the last batter he faced in the eighth inning.

Five days later, he was the starting pitcher on the home U. S. Cellular Field (now Rate Field) mound against the Tampa Bay Rays. The Rays were one of the best teams in Major League Baseball (MLB). They had won the American League (AL) pennant the year before.

Pitcher Mark Buehrle

EXTRA INNINGS

MARK BUEHRLE
PITCHER
WHITE SOX SEASONS: 2000–11
HEIGHT: 6-FOOT-2
WEIGHT: 240 POUNDS
KEY STATS: 5X ALL-STAR, 4X GOLD GLOVE AWARD, 2005 WORLD SERIES CHAMPION, 2X NO-HITTERS (1 PERFECT GAME)

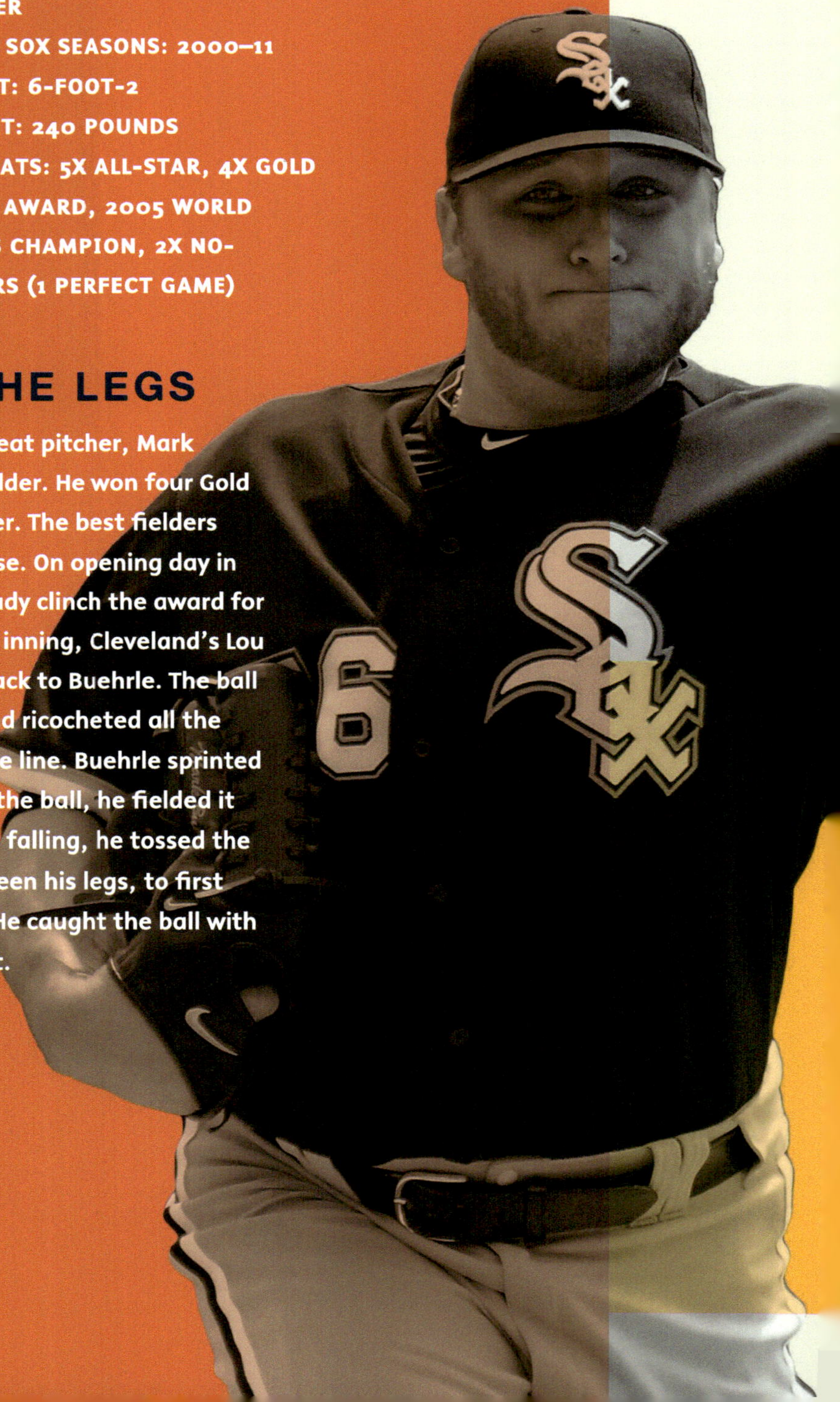

BETWEEN THE LEGS

In addition to being a great pitcher, Mark Buehrle was a terrific fielder. He won four Gold Glove Awards in his career. The best fielders at each position win those. On opening day in 2010, he seemed to already clinch the award for that season. In the fifth inning, Cleveland's Lou Marson hit a grounder back to Buehrle. The ball hit Buehrle's left foot and ricocheted all the way beyond the first base line. Buehrle sprinted after it. When he got to the ball, he fielded it with his glove. As he was falling, he tossed the ball with his glove, between his legs, to first baseman Paul Konerko. He caught the ball with his bare hand for the out.

Chicago skyline

Buehrle easily retired the Rays in the top of the first inning. He got Carlos Peña to pop out on a three-ball count to start the second inning. Buehrle had all the run support he needed in the bottom of the second. With the bases loaded, Josh Fields smashed a grand slam home run over the left field wall. Chicago led 4–0.

Tampa Bay did not come close to getting a hit through eight innings. They were close to getting base runners though. B. J. Upton worked a full count (three balls, two strikes) to lead off the fourth inning. But Buehrle struck him out swinging. Jason Bartlett looked at three balls to start his at-bat in the sixth inning. But he ended up grounding out.

The Rays were retired in order in both the seventh and eighth innings. That set the stage for the ninth inning. Dewayne Wise came in as a defensive replacement in center field for the White Sox to start the inning. Lead-off batter Gabe Kapler for the Rays launched a 2–2 pitch to deep left center. Wise jumped, reached his glove over the fence, brought it back into the field of play, juggled it, and caught it with his left bare hand while falling to the ground. It was one of the greatest fielding plays in MLB history. Buehrle struck out Michel Hernández on a 3–2 count for the next batter. Bartlett then

CHICAGO

grounded out to shortstop Alexei Ramírez to end the game. Twenty-seven up. Twenty-seven down. It was a perfect game! Chicago won 5–0.

Buehrle was still retiring batter after batter during his next start. The White Sox faced the Minnesota Twins in Minneapolis. Buehrle retired the first 17 Twins batters he faced. With two outs in the sixth inning, Twins second baseman Alexi Casilla drew a walk. Buehrle's streak of 45 straight batters retired came to an end. It set a new MLB record that wasn't broken until 2014. He broke the record of 41 by his teammate Bobby Jenks, who had tied the then-record in 2007.

SUCCESS AND SCANDAL

The White Sox franchise has been in existence for more than 120 years. Charles Comiskey owned a minor-league franchise in St. Paul, Minnesota. In 1900, he moved the team to Chicago. It joined the newly formed American League (AL). Comiskey called his team the White Stockings. They soon became known as the White Sox. The following year, the AL elevated itself to major-league status. The White Sox were one of the league's best teams. They won the first AL pennant in 1901. They finished with an 83–53 record. There was no World Series yet. The first one was in 1903. Clark Griffith was the star pitcher and manager of the team. He won 24 games.

The White Sox next won the AL pennant in 1906. They won 93 games. But they had the league's lowest team batting average at .230. They were nicknamed the "Hitless Wonders." Chicago's National League team, the Cubs, won that league's pennant. The Cubs set a major-league record with 116 wins.

Pitcher Eddie Cicotte

The all-Chicago World Series looked to be a mismatch. But it was the White Sox who stunned baseball fans by winning in six games. The Cubs were bitter about the loss. "There is one thing I will never believe," said Cubs manager Frank Chance. "And that is the Sox are better than the Cubs."

Pitcher Ed Walsh won 40 games in 1908. But the offense produced only three home runs all year. The Sox sank in the standings. The team began rebuilding its roster in 1914. Pitcher Urban "Red" Faber came to town. His best pitch was a spitball. (Spitballs were legal in that era.) Another newcomer was outfielder "Shoeless Joe" Jackson. Early in his career, Jackson's shoes gave him blisters during a game. He took them off and played in his socks. A fan shouted, "You shoeless son of a gun!" Jackson never played a game in stocking feet again. But the nickname stuck. Other key additions to the White Sox were second baseman Eddie Collins and pitcher Eddie Cicotte.

In 1917, Chicago won 100 games. The team reached the World Series. It topped the New York Giants in six games. Faber and Cicotte combined to pitch 50 of the total 52 innings in the series.

The White Sox returned to the World Series two years later. This time, they lost to the Cincinnati Reds, five games to three. (From 1919 to 1921, the World Series was a best-of-nine series). Rumors soon began that some Chicago players had thrown the series. Gamblers had made big bets on the outcome. They wanted a sure thing. So they paid the players involved a lot of money to lose. The scandal left a lasting mark on professional baseball. Eight players, including Cicotte and Jackson, became known as the "Black Sox." Many questioned if Jackson was part of the fix. He led the team with 12 hits in the World Series. MLB's first commissioner, Kenesaw Mountain Landis, banned the players for life.

In 1920, the White Sox were poised to take the AL pennant again. But the Black Sox scandal surfaced just before the season ended. Chicago lost its winning edge. Cleveland surpassed the Sox for the pennant. For the rest of the 1920s, the White Sox finished no better than fifth place.

EXTRA INNINGS

IF YOU BUILD IT, HE WILL COME

The 1989 movie *Field of Dreams* is adapted from the novel Shoeless Joe written by W. P. Kinsella. In the movie, Ray Kinsella (played by Kevin Costner), is a farmer in Iowa. While working in his cornfield, he hears a voice that says, "If you build it, he will come." Ray sees a vision of a baseball diamond and of "Shoeless Joe" Jackson (played by Ray Liotta). Ray builds the diamond in his cornfield. The ghost of Jackson arrives. Other ghosts of baseball legends, including members of the "Black Sox" scandal, also arrive at the field and start playing games. It is considered one of the best baseball movies of all time. The movie diamond is a tourist attraction in Dyersville, Iowa.

EXTRA INNINGS

MINNIE MIÑOSO
LEFT FIELDER
WHITE SOX SEASONS: 1951–57, 1960–61, 1964, 1976, 1980
HEIGHT: 5-FOOT-10
WEIGHT: 175 POUNDS
KEY STATS: 2022 HALL OF FAME INDUCTEE, 9X ALL-STAR, 3X GOLD GLOVE AWARD, 3X AL STOLEN BASE LEADER

THIS MINNIE WAS NO MOUSE

Saturnino Orestes Armas Miñoso was born in Cuba in the 1920s. "Minnie" worked in sugar cane fields from a young age. He started a plantation ballclub. His skills earned him a spot on a semi-professional team in 1943. He played in the Negro Leagues for three seasons. The Cleveland Indians signed him in 1949. He joined the White Sox two years later. Fans loved his hustle and enthusiasm. After retiring, Miñoso made several brief returns to the White Sox. He became the third player past the age of 50 to get a hit. He also played in the major leagues in five different decades. Miñoso died in 2015. He was posthumously elected to the Baseball Hall of Fame in 2022.

THE SOX GET GO-GOING

Chicago had just three winning seasons in the 1930s. A rare bright spot was Luke Appling. The young shortstop joined the team in 1930. He had a knack for hitting foul balls. He smacked pitch after pitch until he got a ball he liked. He once hit 17 foul balls in a single at-bat. Then he ripped a triple. Appling was a seven-time All-Star. He played 2,422 games with the Sox. It is still the team record.

The team was even worse during the 1940s. The White Sox produced only two winning seasons. "The whole White Sox squad is up for trade," manager Jimmy Dykes said during one especially poor season. Things improved in the 1950s. The team became known as the "Go-Go Sox." Players hustled on defense. They raced down the base paths. Starting in 1951, Chicago led the AL in stolen bases for 11 straight seasons. The team's nickname could just as easily have come from the way its roster was built. General manager Frank Lane earned the nickname "Trader." Players came and went rapidly.

Second baseman Nellie Fox arrived in 1950. He played for the Sox until 1963. Fox almost never struck out. He led the AL in hits four times. In 1959, he was named the league's Most Valuable Player (MVP).

Left fielder Minnie Miñoso joined the team in 1951. Miñoso was the first Black player to suit up for Chicago. An enthusiastic player, he quickly became a fan favorite. A year later, outfielder Jim Rivera helped kick-start the Sox. He was known for his belly-flopping slides, diving catches, and wild personality. Meanwhile, Billy Pierce led from the mound. "You didn't need a relief pitcher

Pitcher Early Wynn

when he pitched," Lane said of his Go-Go ace. "If he had a one-run lead going into the seventh or eighth inning, the ballgame was over."

Chicago finally started winning games. From 1952 to 1956, it finished third in the AL. Then the White Sox added speedy center fielder Jim Landis and lightning-fast shortstop Luis Aparicio. Aparicio became the team's best base stealer. He led the AL in stolen bases nine straight seasons.

The White Sox rose to second place in 1957 and 1958. The next season, hard-throwing pitcher Early Wynn led them to first place in July. They never gave up the lead. Chicago clinched its first pennant in 40 years. The White Sox gave their all in the World Series. Fox batted .375. First baseman Ted Kluszewski drove in 10 runs. Chicago routed the Los Angeles Dodgers in Game 1. But they won only one more game in the series. Los Angeles won in six games.

First baseman Paul Konerko

DETROIT TIGERS AT
CHICAGO WHITE SOX
JULY 12, 1979

EXTRA INNINGS

DISCO DEMOLITION

Bill Veeck purchased the White Sox in 1975. He had previously owned two MLB teams. He was known for zany promotions. On this night, the White Sox hosted the Detroit Tigers for a doubleheader. In between games, the team held a Disco Demolition Night. Fans who brought disco records could buy tickets to the games for less than a dollar. Records were dumped into bins. They were blown up on the field after the first game. The blaze damaged the Comiskey Park playing surface. Thousands of fans soon swarmed onto the field. Many ripped up chunks of grass. Other fires were lit in the outfield. The field was left unplayable. The White Sox were forced to forfeit the second game.

CONSISTENTLY INCONSISTENT

For the next three decades, the White Sox played some exciting baseball. But they lacked consistency. The team finished the 1964 season with nine straight wins. Chicago finished well again in 1965. Then it began to steadily decline. In 1969, the AL split into two divisions. The Sox were put in the West Division. They lost a franchise-record 106 games in 1970.

The team continued to struggle throughout the 1970s. Despite the challenging seasons, Chicago featured some talented players. First baseman Dick Allen led the AL in 1972 with 37 home runs and 113 runs batted in (RBI). He was named AL MVP. But he was moody. He quit the team with two weeks left in the 1974 season. He later blamed his departure on a feud with another player. Still, he led the AL again with 32 home runs.

On the plus side, Wilbur Wood's knuckleballs baffled opponents. He won 90 games from 1971 to 1974. He led the AL in wins with 24 in 1972 and 1973. The 1977 White Sox became known as the "South Side Hitmen." They slugged a team-record 192 home runs. Designated hitter Oscar Gamble led the way with 31 home runs. Outfielder Richie Zisk slammed 30 more. Third baseman Eric Soderholm added a career-high 25. Still, Chicago finished just third in the division.

In 1983, the White Sox finally topped the AL West. They had 99 wins. It was the most wins since their 1917 world championship season. They qualified for the playoffs for the first time in 24 years. Hard-nosed catcher Carlton Fisk anchored the team. Clutch-hitting right fielder Harold Baines batted in 99 runs. Chicago faced the Baltimore Orioles in the AL Championship Series (ALCS). The Sox won the first game. But they lost the next three in the best-of-five series. Chicago had only one more winning season the rest of the 1980s.

Outfielder Brian Anderson

In 1990, a young White Sox team took the field. They were led by powerful first baseman Frank Thomas. Third baseman Robin Ventura became a dependable hitter. Fiery Jack McDowell was the team's top pitcher. Chicago boasted speed, solid defense, power, and enthusiasm. In 1993, Thomas won the MVP award. McDowell won the Cy Young Award. The White Sox won the AL West. They faced the Toronto Blue Jays in the ALCS. Toronto took the best-of-seven series in six games.

Chicago came back strong the next year. It charged to a 67–46 mark. That led the newly formed AL Central Division. But a players' strike ended the season at that point. The World Series was canceled. Chicago's momentum faded. The Sox climbed no higher than second place for the remainder of the decade.

In 2000, the White Sox re-emerged as an offensive machine. Chicago led the AL in runs scored. It rolled to an AL-best 95–67 record. Five players scored more than 100 runs. Four batted better than .300. But the excitement of the season came to a screeching halt in the AL Division Series (ALDS). The Seattle Mariners swept the Sox in three tight games.

FINALLY, A TITLE

The White Sox hovered near the top of the AL Central for the next four years. They returned to the postseason in 2005. Their playoff appearance surprised many people. The team had followed a "small-ball" strategy. It moved runners along one base at a time. It utilized the depth of its strong pitching staff. Outstanding defense kept games close. The White Sox won the division with 99 wins. That led the AL.

Third baseman Robin Ventura

RIGHT FIELDER HAROLD BAINES

THE NEVER-ENDING GAME

MILWAUKEE BREWERS AT CHICAGO WHITE SOX

MAY 8–9, 1984

This game was so long, it had to be completed over two days. The Brewers and White Sox started on May 8 at Comiskey Park in Chicago, Illinois. The game featured seven future Hall of Famers. Milwaukee scored twice in the top of the ninth to take a 3–1 lead. Chicago countered with two in the bottom half. The game was tied 3-3. Neither team scored through the 17th inning. It was 1 a.m. local time. The game had to be suspended. A rule stated that no new inning could start after that time. It resumed the next day. Both teams scored three runs in the 21st inning. The score was 6–6. In the bottom of the 25th inning, future Hall of Famer Harold Baines put an end to the longest game, in terms of time, in MLB history. He hit a home run to deep center field to give Chicago the 7–6 win. The game lasted eight hours and six minutes.

EXTRA INNINGS

The White Sox dominated the postseason. They won 11 games and lost only once. They swept the Boston Red Sox in the ALDS. Then they knocked off the Los Angeles Angels of Anaheim in five games in the ALCS. All five starting pitchers in the series threw complete games. The White Sox did not use any relief pitchers. It marked the first AL pennant for the Sox since 1959. Chicago continued its dominant postseason run with a sweep of the Houston Astros in the World Series. The White Sox were world champions for the first time in 88 years! "It means a lot not only to us in the clubhouse but to the organization, to the fans, and to the city," said outfielder Jermaine Dye. "It's a great feeling."

The team acquired veteran designated hitter Jim Thome before the 2006 season. But Chicago's title defense fell short. It finished third in the AL Central. In 2008, Chicago tied the Minnesota Twins for first place in the division. A tiebreaker game was needed. It was played in Chicago. Jim Thome's home run in the seventh inning broke a scoreless tie. The run stood up. Chicago won the division. But Tampa Bay knocked them out in the ALDS in four games.

The White Sox went into a long postseason drought after 2008. One bright spot was Cuban first baseman José Abreu. He was named AL Rookie of the Year in 2014. He started his career with four straight 100 RBI seasons. Shortstop Tim Anderson had a breakout year in 2019. He led the majors with a .335 batting average. That was nearly 100 points better than the previous season.

The 2020 season was reduced to just 60 games. The COVID-19 outbreak canceled most of the first four months of the season. The White Sox young talent came together in the shortened season. Abreu had a stellar campaign. He led the AL in hits (76) and all of MLB in RBI (60). He was named AL MVP. The White Sox had their first winning season since 2012. Their 35–25 record qualified them for the

PUTTING ON THE HURT

Frank Thomas led the White Sox resurgence in the early 1990s. It culminated in the 2005 World Series. Thomas was nicknamed "The Big Hurt." He punished opposing pitchers. Thomas is the greatest White Sox hitter ever. He set numerous franchise career batting records. They included home runs, runs scored, total bases, and RBI. Thomas relied on the power generated by his hulking frame. He also had a sharp eye and plenty of patience. Those qualities helped him set a major-league record. He is the only player to earn a batting average of at .300, 20 home runs, 100 RBI, and 100 walks for 7 straight years.

FRANK THOMAS
FIRST BASEMAN
WHITE SOX SEASONS: 1990–2005
HEIGHT: 6-FOOT-5
WEIGHT: 240 POUNDS
KEY STATS: 2014 HALL OF FAME INDUCTEE, 2X AL MVP, 5X ALL-STAR, 521 CAREER HOME RUNS

25

Center fielder Luis Robert Jr.

expanded playoffs as a wild card team. But they lost to the Oakland Athletics in a best-of-three Wild Card series.

Chicago hired Hall of Fame manager Tony La Russa to lead the team in 2021. He managed the team from 1980 to 1986. The Sox won 93 games and won the AL Central. Pitching led the way. Starting pitchers Lance Lynn and Carlos Rodón finished in the top five in AL Cy Young voting. Closer Liam Hendriks led the AL with 38 saves. Houston knocked them out in the ALDS in four games.

The White Sox went into a tailspin. They finished .500 the following season. But they lost 101 games in 2023. The 2024 season was even worse. Three times during the season, they had losing streaks of at least 10 games. Chicago tied an AL record with 21 straight losses. It finished with 121 losses. That set a modern (since 1901) MLB record for losses in a season.

In more than a century of play, the White Sox have given fans heroes and stories worth rooting for. They have also given Chicago three world championships. Fans of the beloved White Sox cannot wait for the day when the winds of fortune blow a fourth title their way.

First baseman Andrew Vaughn

INDEX